KUBERNETES MADE EASY

PANKAJ JOSHI

BLUEROSE PUBLISHERS
India | U.K.

Copyright © Pankaj Joshi 2024

All rights reserved by author. No part of this publication may be reproduced, stored in a retrieval system or transmitted in any form or by any means, electronic, mechanical, photocopying, recording or otherwise, without the prior permission of the author. Although every precaution has been taken to verify the accuracy of the information contained herein, the publisher assumes no responsibility for any errors or omissions. No liability is assumed for damages that may result from the use of information contained within.

BlueRose Publishers takes no responsibility for any damages, losses, or liabilities that may arise from the use or misuse of the information, products, or services provided in this publication.

For permissions requests or inquiries regarding this publication,
please contact:

BLUEROSE PUBLISHERS
www.BlueRoseONE.com
info@bluerosepublishers.com
+91 8882 898 898
+4407342408967

ISBN: 978-93-6452-868-9

Cover Design: Sadhna Kumari
Typesetting: Pooja Sharma

First Edition: October 2024

I thankfully give tribute to Mr Bhupinder Rajput for his work on Kubernetes and wish him all the success in future.

Contents

1. Introduction 1
2. Linux Basics 2
3. Kubernetes Architecture 4
4. Lab Setup 10
5. Pods 13
6. Labels 15
7. Selector 16
8. Replication Controller 18
9. Replica Set 20
10. Deployment Object 22
11. Service 25
12. Volume 27
13. Liveness Probe 33
14. ConfigMap 35
15. Secrets 41
16. Namespace 45
17. Resource Quota 50
18. Horizontal Pod Autoscaling 59
19. Kubernetes Jobs 59
20. Ingress Controller 60
21. HELM Chart 62
22. Kubernetes Migration 64

23. Policies.. 69
24. Kubernetes Security 70
25. Service Mesh... 73

1. Introduction

Kubernetes is a open source platform to manage containerized workloads. It is used to manage Docker containers in the form of a cluster. Along with the automated deployment and scaling of containers, it provides self-healing by automatically restarting failed containers and rescheduling them to other hosts in case if the base host is not available.

It is written in Golang and has vast community as it is developed by Google and later donated to CNCF (Cloud Native Computing Foundation). It has strong community support and works successfully with all Cloud Vendors: Microsoft , AWS, Google Cloud Platform.

2. Linux Basics

Description: In Linux, everything is files, whether it is a hard drive, RAM, Storage, Network Interface etc.

In this tutorial, We will understand few Linux commands:

Users and Groups: Only root or users with sudo privileges can use the useradd command to create new user accounts. When invoked, useradd creates a new user account according to the options specified on the command line and the default values set in the /etc/default/useradd file.

- To list all the users:
- To create a user: useradd <username>
- To list all the groups:
- To create a group:

Password and Policies: useradd also reads the content of the /etc/login.defs file. This file contains configuration for the shadow password suite such as password expiration policy, ranges of user IDs used when creating system and regular users, and more.

- To change the password for the current user: passwd
- To create a user: useradd <username>
- To list all the groups:
- To create a group:

Files and Folders: As we are logged in as current user, we would see the user directories. There are also some directories which are for system usage, so these are called system directories. These are hidden and can be identified with a dot (.) at the start of the directory name.

- To list or find all hidden files, we would explicitly tell the find command to list all files whose names start with a dot (.): find . -name ".*" -maxdepth 1 2> /dev/null

- To check the present working directory: pwd

- To list all the directories (Hidden) in a given path: dir -a

- To list user directories in a given path: dir

- To create a Directory: mkdir <name>

- To delete a Directory and its contents: rm -r <name>

- To check the permission of a Directory: ls -lrtd <name>

- To list the files: ls

- To check the permission of a file: ls -lrt <name>

- To change the permissions of a Directory: chmod xxx <name>

- To change the permissions of a file: chmod xxx <name>

- To create a file: touch <File Name>

- To remove an empty directory using the rm command: rm -d <Directory Name>

- To remove a non-empty directory and its content: rm -r <Directory Name>

- To Ignore any prompt when deleting a write-protected file: rm -f <File Name>

- To Ignore any prompt when deleting a write-protected non-empty folder: rm -rf <Folder Name>

- To delete a working directory and its subdirectories: rmdir -p /Directory/SubDirectory

- To modify the ownership of a file or a directory to another user or group: chown ubuntu:ubuntu hello.txt

3. Kubernetes Architecture

A Kubernetes cluster consists of a control plane plus a set of worker machines, called nodes, that run containerized applications. Every cluster needs at least one worker node in order to run Pods.

The worker node(s) host the Pods that are the components of the application workload. The control plane manages the worker nodes and the Pods in the cluster. In production environments, the control plane usually runs across multiple computers and a cluster usually runs multiple nodes, providing fault-tolerance and high availability.

This document outlines the various components you need to have for a complete and working of Kubernetes cluster.

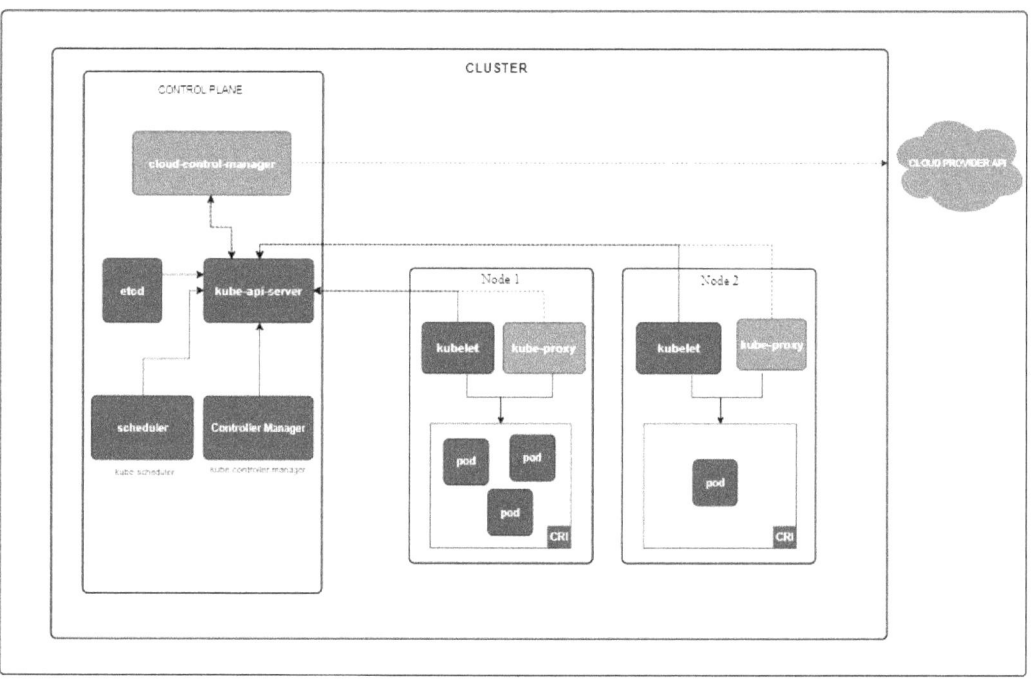

3.1 Kubernetes Cluster Components

3.2 Control Plane Components

The control plane's components make global decisions about the cluster (for example, scheduling), as well as detecting and responding to cluster events (for example, starting up a new pod when a Deployment's replicas field is unsatisfied).

Control plane components can be run on any machine in the cluster. However, for simplicity, setup scripts typically start all control plane components on the same machine, and do not run user containers on this machine. See Creating Highly Available clusters with kubeadm for an example control plane setup that runs across multiple machines.

kube-apiserver: The API server is a component of the Kubernetes control plane that exposes the Kubernetes API. The API server is the front end for the Kubernetes control plane.

The main implementation of a Kubernetes API server is kube-apiserver. kube-apiserver is designed to scale horizontally—that is, it scales by deploying more instances. You can run several instances of kube-apiserver and balance traffic between those instances.

Etcd: Consistent and highly-available key value store used as Kubernetes' backing store for all cluster data. If your Kubernetes cluster uses etcd as its backing store, make sure you have a back up plan for the data. Control plane component that watches for newly created Pods with no assigned node, and selects a node for them to run on.

Kube-Scheduler: Factors taken into account for scheduling decisions include: individual and collective resource requirements, hardware/software/policy constraints, affinity and anti-affinity specifications, data locality, inter-workload interference, and deadlines.

Kube-Controller-Manager: Control plane component that runs controller processes.

Logically, each controller is a separate process, but to reduce complexity, they are all compiled into a single binary and run in a single process. There are many different types of controllers. Some examples of them are:

- **Node Controller:** Responsible for noticing and responding when nodes go down.

- **Job controller:** Watches for Job objects that represent one-off tasks, then creates Pods to run those tasks to completion.

- **EndpointSlice Controller:** Populates EndpointSlice objects (to provide a link between Services and Pods).

- **ServiceAccount Controller:** Create default ServiceAccounts for new namespaces.

Cloud-controller-manager

A Kubernetes control plane component that embeds cloud-specific control logic. The cloud controller manager lets you link your cluster into your cloud provider's API, and separates out the components that interact with that cloud platform from components that only interact with your cluster.

The cloud-controller-manager only runs controllers that are specific to your cloud provider. If you are running Kubernetes on your own premises, or in a learning environment inside your own PC, the cluster does not have a cloud controller manager. As with the kube-controller-manager, the cloud-controller-manager combines several logically independent control loops into a single binary that you run as a single process. You can scale horizontally (run more than one copy) to improve performance or to help tolerate failures.

The following controllers can have cloud provider dependencies:

- **Node controller:** For checking the cloud provider to determine if a node has been deleted in the cloud after it stops responding

- **Route controller:** For setting up routes in the underlying cloud infrastructure

- **Service controller:** For creating, updating and deleting cloud provider load balancers

Node components

Node components run on every node, maintaining running pods and providing the Kubernetes runtime environment.

Kubelet: An agent that runs on each node in the cluster. It makes sure that containers are running in a Pod. The kubelet takes a set of PodSpecs that are provided through various mechanisms and ensures that the containers described in those PodSpecs are running and healthy. The kubelet doesn't manage containers which were not created by Kubernetes.

kube-proxy: kube-proxy is a network proxy that runs on each node in your cluster, implementing part of the Kubernetes Service concept. kube-proxy maintains network rules on nodes. These network rules allow network communication to your Pods from network sessions inside or outside of your cluster. kube-proxy uses the operating system packet filtering layer if there is one and it's available. Otherwise, kube-proxy forwards the traffic itself. If you use a network plugin that implements packet forwarding for Services by itself, and providing equivalent behavior to kube-proxy, then you do not need to run kube-proxy on the nodes in your cluster.

Container runtime: A fundamental component that empowers Kubernetes to run containers effectively. It is responsible for managing the execution and lifecycle of containers within the Kubernetes environment. Kubernetes supports container runtimes such as containerd, CRI-O, and any other implementation of the Kubernetes CRI (Container Runtime Interface).

Addons: Addons use Kubernetes resources (DaemonSet, Deployment, etc) to implement cluster features. Because these are providing cluster-level features, namespaced resources for addons belong within the kube-system namespace. Selected addons are described below; for an extended list of available addons, please see Addons.

DNS: While the other addons are not strictly required, all Kubernetes clusters should have cluster DNS, as many examples rely on it. Cluster DNS is a DNS server, in addition to the other DNS server(s) in your environment, which serves DNS records for Kubernetes services. Containers started by Kubernetes automatically include this DNS server in their DNS searches.

Web UI (Dashboard): Dashboard is a general purpose, web-based UI for Kubernetes clusters. It allows users to manage and troubleshoot applications running in the cluster, as well as the cluster itself.

Container Resource Monitoring: Container Resource Monitoring records generic time-series metrics about containers in a central database, and provides a UI for browsing that data.

Cluster-level Logging: A cluster-level logging mechanism is responsible for saving container logs to a central log store with a search/browsing interface.

Network Plugins: Network plugins are software components that implement the container network interface (CNI) specification. They are responsible for allocating IP addresses to pods and enabling them to communicate with each other within the cluster.

Control plane deployment options

The control plane components can be deployed in several ways:

Traditional deployment: Control plane components run directly on dedicated machines or VMs, often managed as systemd services.

- **Static Pods:** Control plane components are deployed as static Pods, managed by the kubelet on specific nodes. This is a common approach used by tools like kubeadm.

- **Self-hosted:** The control plane runs as Pods within the Kubernetes cluster itself, managed by Deployments and StatefulSets or other Kubernetes primitives.

- **Managed Kubernetes services:** Cloud providers often abstract away the control plane, managing its components as part of their service offering.

Workload Placement Considerations

The placement of workloads, including the control plane components, can vary based on cluster size, performance requirements, and operational policies:

In smaller or development clusters, control plane components and user workloads might run on the same nodes. Larger production clusters often dedicate specific nodes to control plane components, separating them from user workloads. Some organizations run critical add-ons or monitoring tools on control plane nodes.

Cluster Management Tools

Tools like kubeadm, kops, and Kubespray offer different approaches to deploying and managing clusters, each with its own method of component layout and management. The flexibility of Kubernetes architecture allows organizations to tailor their clusters to specific needs, balancing factors such as operational complexity, performance, and management overhead. Customization and extensibility: Kubernetes architecture allows for significant customization: Custom schedulers can be deployed to work alongside the default Kubernetes scheduler or to replace it entirely. API servers can be extended with CustomResourceDefinitions and API Aggregation. Cloud providers can integrate deeply with Kubernetes using the cloud-controller-manager.

4. Lab Setup

1. **Switch to Root user:** sudo su

   ```
   ubuntu@ip-172-31-12-81:~$ sudo su
   root@ip-172-31-12-81:/home/ubuntu#
   ```

2. **Install docker:** sudo apt update && apt -y install docker.io

   ```
   ubuntu@ip-172-31-12-81:~$ sudo su
   root@ip-172-31-12-81:/home/ubuntu# sudo apt update && apt -y install docker.io
   ```

3. **Check Docker Version:** docker --version

   ```
   root@ip-172-31-12-81:/home/ubuntu# docker --version
   Docker version 20.10.21, build 20.10.21-0ubuntu1~22.04.3
   root@ip-172-31-12-81:/home/ubuntu#
   ```

4. **Install Kubectl (Third-Party):** curl -LO https://storage.googleapis.com/kubernetes-release/release/$(curl -s https://storage.googleapis.com/kubernetes-release/release/stable.txt)/bin/linux/amd64/kubectl && chmod +x ./kubectl && sudo mv ./kubectl /usr/local/bin/kubectl

5. **Install Kubectl (Official):** curl -LO https://dl.k8s.io/release/$(curl -L -s https://dl.k8s.io/release/stable.txt)/bin/linux/amd64/kubectl

Ref: https://kubernetes.io/docs/tasks/tools/install-kubectl-linux/

6. Check Kubectl Server Version: kubectl version --client

Execute the below commands as well:

7. **Clone Brew Repository:** git clone https://github.com/Homebrew/brew homebrew

8. **Install Brew:** eval "$(homebrew/bin/brew shellenv)" && brew update --force --quiet && chmod -R go-w "$(brew --prefix)/share/zsh"

9. **Install Minikube:** brew install minikube

10. **Install GCC:** brew install gcc

11. **Start the cluster using docker driver:** minikube start –driver=docker

```
root@ip-172-31-1-65:/home/ubuntu/cri-dockerd# install packaging/systemd/* /etc/systemd/system
root@ip-172-31-1-65:/home/ubuntu/cri-dockerd# sed -i -e 's,/usr/bin/cri-dockerd,/usr/local/bin/cri-dockerd,' /etc/systemd/system/cri-docker.service
root@ip-172-31-1-65:/home/ubuntu/cri-dockerd# systemctl daemon-reload
root@ip-172-31-1-65:/home/ubuntu/cri-dockerd# systemctl enable cri-docker.service
Created symlink /etc/systemd/system/multi-user.target.wants/cri-docker.service → /etc/systemd/system/cri-docker.service.
root@ip-172-31-1-65:/home/ubuntu/cri-dockerd# systemctl enable --now cri-docker.socket
Created symlink /etc/systemd/system/sockets.target.wants/cri-docker.socket → /etc/systemd/system/cri-docker.socket.
root@ip-172-31-1-65:/home/ubuntu/cri-dockerd#
```

```
root@ip-172-31-1-65:/home/ubuntu# curl -LO https://storage.googleapis.com/minikube/releases/latest/minikube-linux-amd64
  % Total    % Received % Xferd  Average Speed   Time    Time     Time  Current
                                 Dload  Upload   Total   Spent    Left  Speed
100 80.0M  100 80.0M    0     0  11.5M      0  0:00:06  0:00:06 --:--:-- 16.4M
root@ip-172-31-1-65:/home/ubuntu# sudo install minikube-linux-amd64 /usr/local/bin/minikube
root@ip-172-31-1-65:/home/ubuntu#
```

12. Install Conntrack: apt install conntrack

```
root@ip-172-31-10-221:/home/ubuntu# apt install conntrack
Reading package lists... Done
Building dependency tree... Done
Reading state information... Done
conntrack is already the newest version (1:1.4.6-2build2).
0 upgraded, 0 newly installed, 0 to remove and 70 not upgraded.
root@ip-172-31-10-221:/home/ubuntu#
```

5. Pods

Description: PODS are the basic building block of a Kubernetes Deployment. PODS execute the O/s Images which are called Containers.

Commands

1. To clear the screen <ctrl+l)
2. Install Curl:
   - apt update && apt upgrade
   - apt install curl
3. To list all the resources in the kubernetes cluster: kubectl get all
4. To create a YAML file:

   Open vi Editor: vi pod1.yaml

   To exit the vi Editor, press "shift" key and type ":wq"
5. To Delete a yaml file: rm -rf myrc.yaml
6. To Create a POD from YAML file: kubectl apply -f <file>.yaml
7. To View the pods with details: kubectl get pods -o wide
8. To Delete a Pod: kubectl delete pods <podname>
9. To view the pod details: Kubectl describe pods <pod name>
10. To enter in a POD: kubectl exec <file name> -it -c <pod name> -- /bin/bash
11. To exit out of a POD: exit

Syntax

apiVersion: v1

kind: Pod

metadata:

 name: pod1

 labels:

   app: tomcat

spec:

 containers:

 - name: tomcat

   image: tomcat

   ports:

    - containerPort: 8080

6. Labels

Description

Labels are Key/Value pairs that are attached to objects, such as PODS.

Commands

1. To create a label: kubectl label pods <pod-name> Environment=Production
2. To view all the labels: kubectl get pods --show-labels
3. To Apply the Label on POD: kubectl label pods <podname> key=value
4. To Apply the Label on Node: kubectl label nodes <nodename> key=value
5. To View the pods with label: kubectl get pods -l key=value
6. To Delete a POD with Label: kubectl delete pods -l key=value

Syntax:

kind: Pod

apiVersion: v1

metadata:

 name: delhipod

 labels:

  name: development

  class: pods

spec:

 containers:

  - name: c00

   image: ubuntu

   command: ["/bin/bash", "-c", "while true; do echo Hello-Pankaj; sleep 5 ; done"]

7. Selector

Description

Labels selector is an object in Kubernetes which is used to group pods with similar function (task). So, they are used by the users to select a set of objects. Kubernetes currently supports two type of selectors – Equality-based selectors. Set-based selectors.

Commands

1. To list pods matching a label: kubectl get pods -l Environment=Production

2. To list where "Production" Label is not present: kubectl get pods -l Environment!=Production

3. To delete a Pod using Label: kubectl delete pod -l Environemnt=POC

Examples:

- Name   Pankaj
- Class   Nodes
- Project Development

4. Set Based Labels: (in, notin and exists)

5. env in (production, dev)

6. env notin (team1, team2)

7. Examples: kubectl get pods -l 'env in (development, testing)'

8. kubectl get pods -l 'env notin (development, testing)'

Syntax

kind: Pod

apiVersion: v1

metadata:

  name: nodelabels

  labels:

    env: development

spec:

  containers:

    - name: c00

      image: ubuntu

      command: ["/bin/bash", "-c", "while true; do echo Hello; sleep 5; done"]

  nodeSelector:

    hardware: t2-medium

8. Replication Controller

Description

A ReplicationController ensures that a specified number of pod replicas are running at any one time. In other words, a ReplicationController makes sure that a pod or a set of similar pods is always up and available.

Commands

1. To view Replication Controller names: kubectl get rc

2. To view Replication Controller details: kubectl describe rc <rc name>

3. To scale up or scale down the RC pods: kubectl scale --replicas=5 rc -l myname=Pankaj

Syntax

kind: ReplicationController

apiVersion: v1

metadata:

  name: myreplica

spec:

  replicas: 2

  selector:

    myname: Pankaj Joshi

  template:

    metadata:

      name: testpod6

      labels:

```
    myname: Pankaj
  spec:
   containers:
    - name: c00
      image: ubuntu
      command: ["/bin/bash", "-c", "while true; do echo Hello; sleep 5 ; done"]
```

9. Replica Set

Description

Replication Controller works only on equality based Selectors, whereas Replica Set works both on equality based and set based Selectors.

Commands

1. To view Replica Set: kubectl get rs
2. To Delete a Replica set: kubectl delete rs <replica set name>
3. To scale up or scale down the RC pods: kubectl scale --replicass=1 rs/myrs

Syntax

kind: ReplicaSet

apiVersion: apps/v1

metadata:

  name: myrs

spec:

  replicas: 2

  selector:

    matchExpressions: # these must match the labels

      - {key: myname, operator: In, values: [Narender, Narendra]}

      - {key: env, operator: NotIn, values: [production]}

  template:

    metadata:

      name: testpod7

      labels:

```
    myname: Pankaj Joshi
  spec:
   containers:
    - name: c00
      image: ubuntu
      command: ["/bin/bash", "-c", "while true; do echo Hello World; sleep 5 ; done"]
```

10. Deployment Object

Description

We use Deployment object to Rollout, Rollback an application via ReplicaSet. It acts a supervisor for pods but manages it via ReplicaSet. If we have 3 replica sets (v1, v2,v3), and we have presently roll-out v3, we can rollback to v1 or v2 via Deployment Object. The Replica Set creates the Pods and checks the status of the Roll-out(s).

Failed Deployments:

1. Insufficient Quotas
2. Readiness Probe Failures
3. Image Pull Errors
4. Insufficient Permission
5. Limit Ranges
6. Application Runtime Misconfiguration

Commands

1. To Rollback updates: kubectl rollout undo deploy/mydeployments --to-revision=2
2. To inspect the deployment in the cluster: kubectl get deploy
3. The following fields are displayed
   - NAME: List the names of the deployments in the namespace.
   - READY: Display how many replicas of the application are available to your users.
   - UP-TO-DATE: Display the number of replicas that has been updated to achieve the desired state.

- AVAILABLE: Displays how many replicas of the application are available to the users.
- AGE: Displays the amount of time that the application has been running.

4. To check whether deployment was created: kubectl get deploy
5. To check how deployment creates Replica Set & Pods: kubectl describe deploy mydeployments
6. kubectl get rs
7. kubectl scale --replicas=4 deploy mydeployments
8. To check what is running inside containers: kubectl logs -f <podname>
9. To exit from Screen Output , ctrl + c / ctrl + z
10. To check the rollout status: kubectl rollout status deployment mydeployments
11. To check the rollout versions: kubectl rollout history deployment mydeployments
12. kubectl rollout undo deploy/mydeployments
13. To delete Deployment Object: kubectl delete deployment mydeployments

Syntax

kind: Deployment

apiVersion: apps/v1

metadata:

  name: mydeployments

spec:

  replicas: 2

  selector:

   matchLabels:

    name: deployment

```
template:
  metadata:
    name: testpod
    labels:
      name: deployment
  spec:
   containers:
    - name: c00
      image: ubuntu
      command: ["/bin/bash", "-c", "while true; do echo Hello World; sleep 5; done"]
```

11. Service

Description

Service object is used to expose an application to the internet. A Virtual Ip (VIP) is used to map to the ip of the individual pods that runs the application. So, service object is used to expose the VIP mapped to the PODS and allows application to receive traffic. Labels are used to select which are the pods to be put under a service. Creating a Service will create an end-point to access the PODS/Application in it.

Services can be exposed in different ways by specifying a type in the service specification:

1. Cluster IP: It is used for pod to pod communication within the same cluster. This means that a client running outside of the cluster, such as a user accessing an application over the internet, cannot directly access a ClusterIP Service.

   When a ClusterIP Service is created, it is assigned a static IP address. This address remains the same for the lifetime of the Service. When a client sends a request to the IP address, the request is automatically routed to one of the Pods behind the Service. If multiple Pods are associated, the ClusterIP Service uses load balancing to distribute traffic equally among them.

2. NodePort: The NodePort Service is a way to expose your application to external clients. An external client is anyone who is trying to access your application from outside of the Kubernetes cluster. The NodePort Service does this by opening the port you choose (in the range of 30000 to 32767) on all worker nodes in the cluster. This port is what external clients will use to connect to your app. So, if the nodePort is set to 30020, for example, anyone who wants to use your app can just connect to any worker node's IP address, on port :30020

3. Load Balancer: A LoadBalancer Service is another way you can expose your applications to external clients. However, it only works if you're using Kubernetes on a cloud platform that supports this Service type.

4. Ingress: Advanced routing and multi-service exposure with added complexity.

Commands

- To list the service Objects: Kubectl get svc
- To list the service including system pods: Kubectl get svc -A
- To delete a service: kubectl delete service <service name>
- To Describe a Service: kubectl describe service <service name>

Syntax

kind: Service   # Defines to create Service type Object

apiVersion: v1

metadata:

name: SampleService

spec:

ports:

- port: 80   # Containers port exposed

targetPort: 80   # Pods port

selector:

name: deployment label   # Apply this service to any pods which has the specific

type: ClusterIP   # Specifies the service type i.e ClusterIP or NodePort

12. Volume

Description: Containers are short lived so if a container is deleted, all the data stored in a container is deleted as well. To overcome this problem, Kubernetes uses Volumes. The storage medium and its content type are determined by the volume type.

In Kubernetes, a volume is attached to a POD and shared among the containers of that POD. The volume has the same life span as that of a POD, which means it gets deleted with the POD.

A volume type decides the properties of a directory, like Size, Content etc.

- Node-Local: It is attached to a Node in which we can create an Empty Directory or a Host Path.
- File Sharing Types: Such as NFS
- Cloud Provider Specific Types: Such as Amazon Elastic Block Store, Azure Disk etc
- Distributed File System Types: Such as Glusterfs, CephFS
- Special Purpose Types: Secret, GitRepo

EmptyDir: Use this when we want to share content between multiple containers on the same POD and not to the host machine. An EmptyDir lives and dies with the Pod. The volume gets re-created when a POD is re-created. However, if a container gets deleted, the Volume will still exists.

HostPath: Use this when we want to access the content of a Pod, Container from Host Machine (Node). A HostPath volume mounts a file or directory from the host node's filesystem into your Pod. In other words, container's storage is mapped to Host's Storage.

Persistent Volume: It is a cluster wide resource that you can use to store data in way that it persists beyond the lifetime of a Pod. The PV is backed by an EBS or NFS. In order to use PV, we need to claim it by using Persistent Volume Claim. The Persistent Volume can be released once the user finishes his work. The underlying PV can be re-claimed for future use.

Commands:

To create a file: echo "Hello World" >file1.txt

To check the file details in a directory: ll /tmp

To access the volume: kubectl exec myvolhostpath -- ls /tmp/hostpath

Syntax:

=========================

EmptyDir

=========================

apiVersion: v1

kind: Pod

metadata:

  name: myvolemptydir

spec:

  containers:

  - name: c1

    image: centos

    command: ["/bin/bash", "-c", "sleep 15000"]

    volumeMounts: # Mount definition inside the container

      - name: xchange

        mountPath: "/tmp/xchange"

```
  - name: c2
    image: centos
    command: ["/bin/bash", "-c", "sleep 10000"]
    volumeMounts:
      - name: xchange
        mountPath: "/tmp/data"
  volumes:
  - name: xchange
    emptyDir: {}
```

========================

HOST PATH

========================

```
apiVersion: v1
kind: Pod
metadata:
  name: myvolhostpath
spec:
  containers:
  - image: centos
    name: testc
    command: ["/bin/bash", "-c", "sleep 15000"]
    volumeMounts:
    - mountPath: /tmp/hostpath
      name: testvolume
```

```
  volumes:
   - name: testvolume
     hostPath:
       path: /tmp/data
```

========================

Persistent Volume

========================

```
apiVersion: v1
kind: PersistentVolume
metadata:
  name: myebsvol
spec:
  capacity:
    storage: 1Gi
  accessModes:
    - ReadWriteOnce
  persistentVolumeReclaimPolicy: Recycle
  awsElasticBlockStore:
    volumeID: vol-0f7f7b07b4d258e22       # YAHAN APNI EBS VOLUME ID DAALO
    fsType: ext4
```

========================

Persistent Volume Claim-1

========================

Description:

Commands:

1. To view the Persistent Volumes: kubectl get pv

apiVersion: v1

kind: PersistentVolumeClaim

metadata:

  name: myebsvolclaim

spec:

  accessModes:

    - ReadWriteOnce

  resources:

    requests:

      storage: 1Gi

========================

Persistent Volume Claim -2

========================

Commands:

1. Kubectl get deploy

Syntax:

apiVersion: apps/v1

kind: Deployment

metadata:

```
    name: pvdeploy
spec:
  replicas: 1
  selector:      # tells the controller which pods to watch/belong to
    matchLabels:
     app: mypv
  template:
    metadata:
      labels:
        app: mypv
    spec:
      containers:
      - name: shell
        image: centos
        command: ["bin/bash", "-c", "sleep 10000"]
        volumeMounts:
        - name: mypd
          mountPath: "/tmp/persistent"
      volumes:
      - name: mypd
        persistentVolumeClaim:
          claimName: myebsvolclaim
```

```
root@Master:/home/ubuntu# kubectl get pods
NAME                       READY   STATUS    RESTARTS   AGE
pvdeploy-f74845446-k4xtf   1/1     Running   0          4m7s
root@Master:/home/ubuntu# kubectl exec pvdeploy-f74845446-k4xtf -it -- /bin/bash
[root@pvdeploy-f74845446-k4xtf /]#
```

13. Liveness Probe

Description: It is a mechanism in which we can check if the application in the container is working as expected. It has 3 parameters:

1. InitialDelaySeconds: It is the time which is taken for the container and the application inside it to get started, once the POD is ready, automatic probe will begin.

2. PeriodSeconds: It is the time interval between each probe.

3. TimeOutSeconds: It is the time taken to get the response of a proble. If we do not get a response till TimeOutSeconds, the container will be restarted.

Commands:

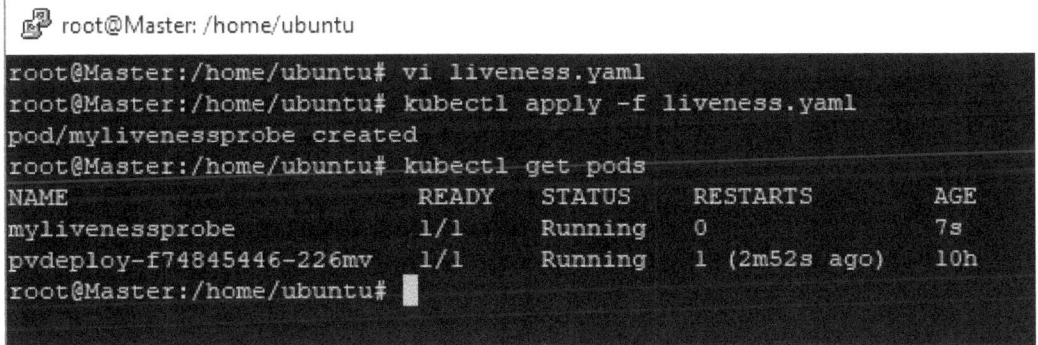

Syntax

apiVersion: v1

kind: Pod

metadata:

  labels:

    test: liveness

  name: mylivenessprobe

```
spec:
  containers:
  - name: liveness
    image: ubuntu
    args:
    - /bin/sh
    - -c
    - touch /tmp/healthy; sleep 1000
    livenessProbe:
      exec:
        command:
        - cat
        - /tmp/healthy
      initialDelaySeconds: 5
      periodSeconds: 5
      timeoutSeconds: 30
```

Note* To check if the liveness probe is working as expected. If we get 0, it means the container is ready, else for non-zero values, the container is not ready.

1. Kubectl exec <podname> -it -- /bin/bash
2. Cat /tm/healthy
3. Echo $?

```
root@mylivenessprobe: /
root@Master:/home/ubuntu# kubectl exec mylivenessprobe -it -- /bin/bash
root@mylivenessprobe:/# cat /tmp/healthy
root@mylivenessprobe:/# echo $?
0
root@mylivenessprobe:/#
```

14. ConfigMap

Description: It maintains the configuration files in Virtual Memory (EBS). The file gets copied to the Volume of the respective Nodes and from there, it is stored in each containers where it is required.

Commands:

1. **To create a sample file**: vi sample.conf
2. **To create a ConfigMap**: kubectl create configmap mymap –from-file=sample.config

"kubectl create configmap <object-name> --from-file=<Configuration file name>

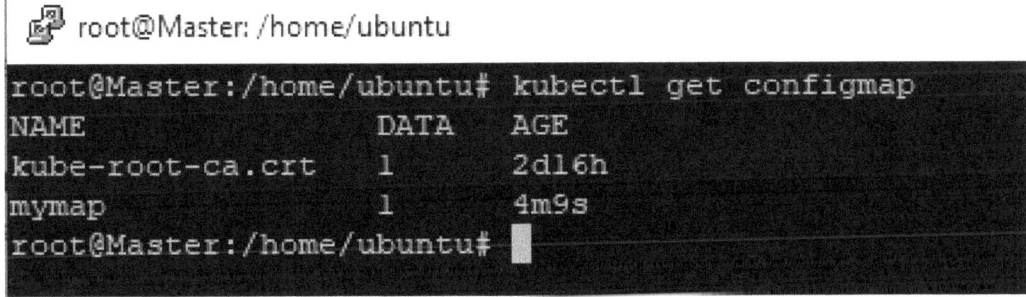

3. **To view the configmap objects**: kubectl get configmap

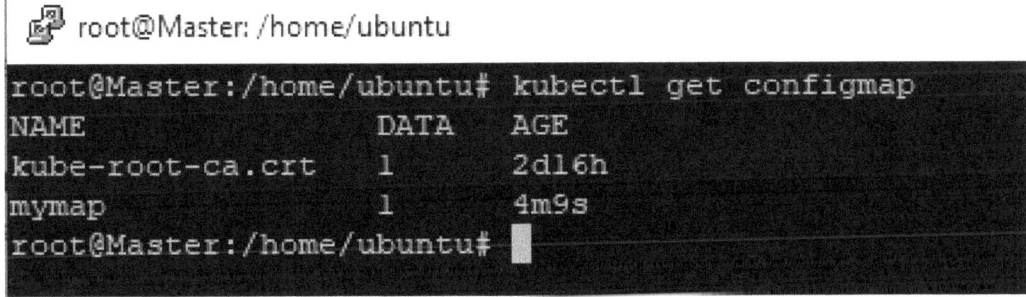

4. **To check the details of the configmap**: kubectl describe configmap mymap

```
root@Master:/home/ubuntu# kubectl get configmap
NAME                 DATA   AGE
kube-root-ca.crt     1      2d16h
mymap                1      4m9s
root@Master:/home/ubuntu# kubectl describe configmap mymap
Name:         mymap
Namespace:    default
Labels:       <none>
Annotations:  <none>

Data
====
sample.conf:
----
This is my configuration file for any application


BinaryData
====

Events:  <none>
root@Master:/home/ubuntu#
```

Syntax:

==============================

Configmap via Volume

==============================

 apiVersion: v1

kind: Pod

metadata:

  name: myvolconfig

spec:

  containers:

- name: c1

     image: centos

   command: ["/bin/bash", "-c", "while true; do echo Technical-Guftgu; sleep 5 ; done"]

     volumeMounts:

      - name: testconfigmap

        mountPath: "/tmp/config"   # the config files will be mounted as ReadOnly by default here

   volumes:

   - name: testconfigmap

     configMap:

       name: mymap   # this should match the config map name created in the first step

       items:

       - key: sample.conf

         path: sample.conf

```
root@Master: /home/ubuntu
ubuntu@Master:~$ sudo su
root@Master:/home/ubuntu# minikube status
minikube
type: Control Plane
host: Running
kubelet: Running
apiserver: Running
kubeconfig: Configured

root@Master:/home/ubuntu# kubectl get configmap
NAME                DATA   AGE
kube-root-ca.crt    1      2d17h
mymap               1      104m
root@Master:/home/ubuntu# vi deployconfigmap.yaml
root@Master:/home/ubuntu#
```

```
root@Master:/home/ubuntu# kubectl apply -f deployconfigmap.yaml
pod/myvolconfig configured
root@Master:/home/ubuntu#
```

```
root@Master:/home/ubuntu# kubectl apply -f deployconfigmap.yaml
pod/myvolconfig configured
root@Master:/home/ubuntu# kubectl get pods
NAME                          READY   STATUS    RESTARTS       AGE
mylivenessprobe               1/1     Running   14 (3m27s ago) 2d5h
myvolconfig                   1/1     Running   0              56s
pvdeploy-f74845446-226mv      1/1     Running   3 (121m ago)   2d15h
root@Master:/home/ubuntu# kubectl exec myvolconfig -it -- /bin/bash
[root@myvolconfig /]# cd /tmp
[root@myvolconfig tmp]# ls
config  ks-script-4luisyla  ks-script-o23i7rc2  ks-script-x6ei4wuu
[root@myvolconfig tmp]# ls -l
total 16
drwxrwxrwx 3 root root 4096 May 18 09:29 config
-rwx------ 1 root root  701 Sep 15  2021 ks-script-4luisyla
-rwx------ 1 root root  671 Sep 15  2021 ks-script-o23i7rc2
-rwx------ 1 root root  291 Sep 15  2021 ks-script-x6ei4wuu
[root@myvolconfig tmp]# cd config
[root@myvolconfig config]# ls
sample.conf
[root@myvolconfig config]# cat sample.conf
This is my configuration file for any application
[root@myvolconfig config]#
```

===============================

Configmap via Environment Variable

===============================

apiVersion: v1

kind: Pod

metadata:

 name: myenvconfig

spec:

 containers:

 - name: c1

    image: centos

    command: ["/bin/bash", "-c", "while true; do echo Technical-Guftgu; sleep 5 ; done"]

    env:

    - name: MYENV   # env name in which value of the key is stored

      valueFrom:

        configMapKeyRef:

          name: mymap   # name of the config created

          key: sample.conf

1. Create a yaml file: vi deployenv.yaml
2. Create a pod with deployenv.yaml: kubectl apply -f deployenv.yaml

```
root@Master:/home/ubuntu# vi deployenv.yaml
root@Master:/home/ubuntu# kubectl apply -f deployenv.yaml
pod/myenvconfig created
root@Master:/home/ubuntu#
```

3. Check if the pod is listed: kubectl get pods

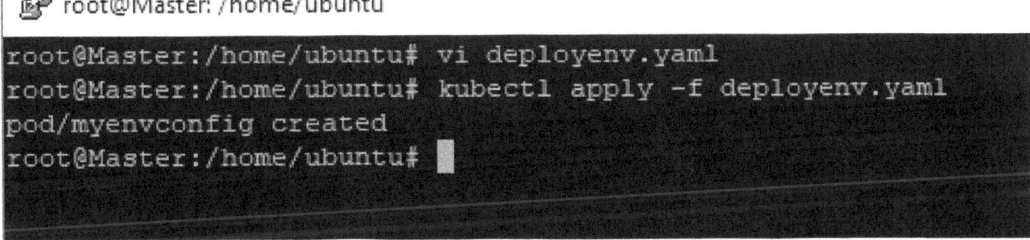

```
root@Master:/home/ubuntu# vi deployenv.yaml
root@Master:/home/ubuntu# kubectl apply -f deployenv.yaml
pod/myenvconfig created
root@Master:/home/ubuntu# kubectl get pods
NAME                         READY   STATUS    RESTARTS       AGE
myenvconfig                  1/1     Running   0              2m55s
mylivenessprobe              1/1     Running   14 (13m ago)   2d5h
myvolconfig                  1/1     Running   0              10m
pvdeploy-f74845446-226mv     1/1     Running   3 (130m ago)   2d16h
```

4. Enter in the pod: kubectl exec myenvconfig -it -- /bin/bash

```
root@Master:/home/ubuntu# vi deployenv.yaml
root@Master:/home/ubuntu# kubectl apply -f deployenv.yaml
pod/myenvconfig created
root@Master:/home/ubuntu# kubectl get pods
NAME                         READY   STATUS    RESTARTS        AGE
myenvconfig                  1/1     Running   0               2m55s
mylivenessprobe              1/1     Running   14 (13m ago)    2d5h
myvolconfig                  1/1     Running   0               10m
pvdeploy-f74845446-226mv     1/1     Running   3 (130m ago)    2d16h
root@Master:/home/ubuntu# kubectl exec myenvconfig -it -- /bin/bash
[root@myenvconfig /]# cd /tmp
[root@myenvconfig tmp]# ls
ks-script-4luisyla  ks-script-o23i7rc2  ks-script-x6ei4wuu
[root@myenvconfig tmp]#
```

5. List the details of the Environment Variable: env

```
root@Master:/home/ubuntu# kubectl exec myenvconfig -it -- /bin/bash
[root@myenvconfig /]# env
LANG=en_US.UTF-8
HOSTNAME=myenvconfig
MYENV=This is my configuration file for any application
KUBERNETES_PORT_443_TCP_PROTO=tcp
KUBERNETES_PORT_443_TCP_ADDR=10.96.0.1
KUBERNETES_PORT=tcp://10.96.0.1:443
PWD=/
HOME=/root
KUBERNETES_SERVICE_PORT_HTTPS=443
KUBERNETES_PORT_443_TCP_PORT=443
KUBERNETES_PORT_443_TCP=tcp://10.96.0.1:443
TERM=xterm
SHLVL=1
KUBERNETES_SERVICE_PORT=443
PATH=/usr/local/sbin:/usr/local/bin:/usr/sbin:/usr/bin:/sbin:/bin
KUBERNETES_SERVICE_HOST=10.96.0.1
LESSOPEN=||/usr/bin/lesspipe.sh %s
_=/usr/bin/env
[root@myenvconfig /]#
```

15. Secrets

Description: It maintains the sensitive data (Credentials, Certificates) or the information exactly like ConfigMap. The file gets copied to the Volume of the respective Nodes and from there, it is stored in each container's where it is required.

Commands:

1. Create a file for username and password

2. Create a Secret: kubectl create secret generic mysecret --from-file=username.txt –from-file=password.txt

3. Check if the secret is created

4. Check if we are able to view the contents of "mysecret"

```
root@Master:/home/ubuntu# kubectl create secret generic mysecret --from-file=username.txt --from-file=password.txt
secret/mysecret created
root@Master:/home/ubuntu# kubectl get secret
NAME       TYPE     DATA   AGE
mysecret   Opaque   2      88s
root@Master:/home/ubuntu# kubectl describe secret mysecret
Name:         mysecret
Namespace:    default
Labels:       <none>
Annotations:  <none>

Type:  Opaque

Data
====
username.txt:  5 bytes
password.txt:  14 bytes
root@Master:/home/ubuntu#
```

Syntax:

apiVersion: v1

kind: Pod

metadata:

  name: myvolsecret

spec:

  containers:

  - name: c1

    image: centos

    command: ["/bin/bash", "-c", "while true; do echo Technical-guftgu; sleep 5 ; done"]

    volumeMounts:

     - name: testsecret

      mountPath: "/tmp/mysecrets"   # the secret files will be mounted as ReadOnly by default here

  volumes:

  - name: testsecret

    secret:

      secretName: mysecret

1. Create a yaml file : vi deploysecret.yaml

2. Create a pod: kubectl apply -f deploysecret.yaml

```
root@Master:/home/ubuntu# vi deploysecret.yaml
root@Master:/home/ubuntu# kubectl apply -f deploysecret.yaml
pod/myvolsecret created
root@Master:/home/ubuntu#
```

3. Check if the pod is created: kubectl get pods

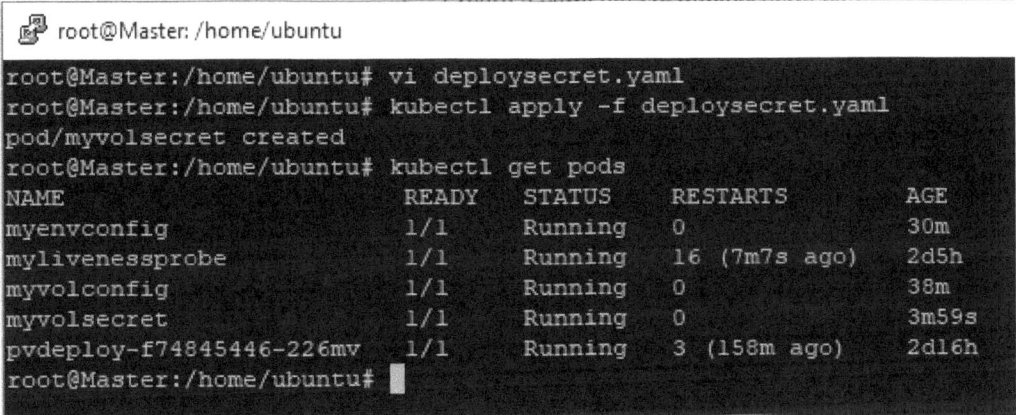

4. Enter in the pod: kubectl exec myvolsecret -it -- /bin/bash

Enter the /tmp directory

Note* We would find "mysecrets" directory

```
root@Master:/home/ubuntu# vi deploysecret.yaml
root@Master:/home/ubuntu# kubectl apply -f deploysecret.yaml
pod/myvolsecret created
root@Master:/home/ubuntu# kubectl get pods
NAME                         READY    STATUS     RESTARTS         AGE
myenvconfig                  1/1      Running    0                30m
mylivenessprobe              1/1      Running    16 (7m7s ago)    2d5h
myvolconfig                  1/1      Running    0                38m
myvolsecret                  1/1      Running    0                3m59s
pvdeploy-f74845446-226mv     1/1      Running    3 (158m ago)     2d16h
root@Master:/home/ubuntu# kubectl exec myvolsecret -it -- /bin/bash
[root@myvolsecret /]# cd /tmp
[root@myvolsecret tmp]# ls
ks-script-4luisyla  ks-script-o23i7rc2  ks-script-x6ei4wuu  mysecrets
```

```
root@Master:/home/ubuntu# kubectl exec myvolsecret -it -- /bin/bash
[root@myvolsecret /]# cd /tmp
[root@myvolsecret tmp]# cd mysecrets
[root@myvolsecret mysecrets]# ls
password.txt  username.txt
[root@myvolsecret mysecrets]# cat password.txt
mypassword123
[root@myvolsecret mysecrets]# cat username.txt
root
[root@myvolsecret mysecrets]#
```

16. Namespace

Description: Namespace is a folder to organize projects.

Commands:

1. To view the namespaces: kubectl get namespaces

```
root@Master:/home/ubuntu# kubectl get namespaces
NAME              STATUS   AGE
default           Active   3d7h
kube-node-lease   Active   3d7h
kube-public       Active   3d7h
kube-system       Active   3d7h
root@Master:/home/ubuntu#
```

2. To list the pods in a namespace: kubectl get pods -n <namespace>

```
root@Master:/home/ubuntu# kubectl get pods -n default
NAME                       READY   STATUS    RESTARTS        AGE
myenvconfig                1/1     Running   1 (9m3s ago)    13h
mylivenessprobe            1/1     Running   17 (13h ago)    2d18h
myvolconfig                1/1     Running   1 (9m3s ago)    13h
myvolsecret                1/1     Running   1 (9m3s ago)    13h
pvdeploy-f74845446-226mv   1/1     Running   4 (9m3s ago)    3d5h
root@Master:/home/ubuntu#
```

3. To view the details of a namespace: kubectl describe namespace <namespace>

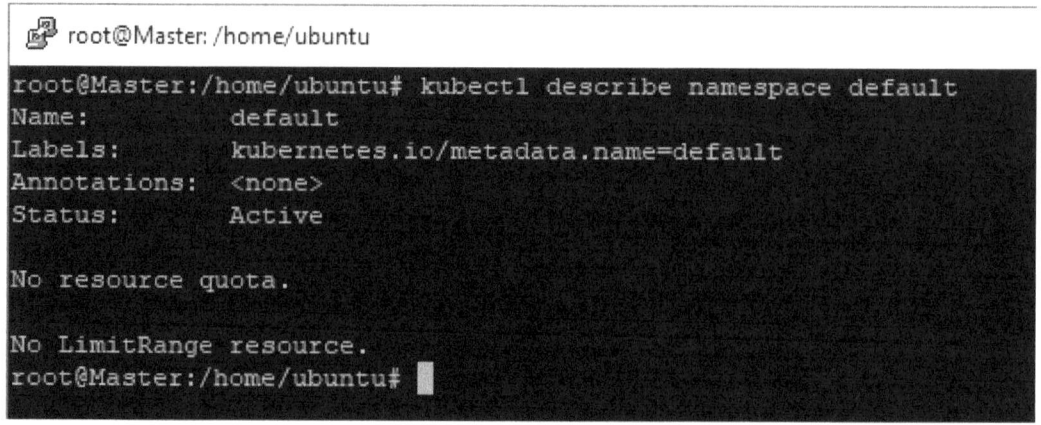

4. To create a namespace: kubectl create namespace POC

Syntax:

====================================

Namespace Creation

====================================

apiVersion: v1

kind: Namespace

metadata:

  name: dev

labels:

name: dev

1. Create a yaml file for dev namespace: vi devns.yaml
2. Create a pod: kubectl apply -f devns.yaml

```
root@Master:/home/ubuntu# vi devns.yaml
root@Master:/home/ubuntu# kubectl apply -f devns.yaml
namespace/dev created
root@Master:/home/ubuntu#
```

3. Create a yaml file for production namespace: vi prodns.yaml
4. Create a prod: kubectl apply -f prodns.yaml

```
root@Master:/home/ubuntu# vi prodns.yaml
root@Master:/home/ubuntu# kubectl apply -f prodns.yaml
namespace/prod unchanged
root@Master:/home/ubuntu# kubectl get ns
NAME              STATUS   AGE
default           Active   3d8h
dev               Active   6m3s
kube-node-lease   Active   3d8h
kube-public       Active   3d8h
kube-system       Active   3d8h
prod              Active   2m10s
root@Master:/home/ubuntu#
```

5. To view the newly created namespace: kubectl get namespace

```
root@Master:/home/ubuntu# kubectl get namespace
NAME              STATUS   AGE
default           Active   3d8h
dev               Active   8m25s
kube-node-lease   Active   3d8h
kube-public       Active   3d8h
kube-system       Active   3d8h
prod              Active   4m32s
root@Master:/home/ubuntu#
```

======================

POD

======================

Command:

1. Create a yaml file for a new pod: vi pod.yaml

kind: Pod

apiVersion: v1

metadata:

  name: testpod

spec:

  containers:

    - name: c00

      image: ubuntu

      command: ["/bin/bash", "-c", "while true; do echo Technical Guftgu; sleep 5 ; done"]

  restartPolicy: Never

2. Create the pod in the desired namespace: kubectl apply -f pod.yaml -n dev

```
root@Master:/home/ubuntu# kubectl apply -f pod.yaml -n dev
pod/testpod created
root@Master:/home/ubuntu# kubectl get pods -n dev
NAME       READY   STATUS    RESTARTS   AGE
testpod    1/1     Running   0          8s
root@Master:/home/ubuntu#
```

3. To delete the pod in the specified namespace: kubectl delete pods testpod -n dev

```
root@Master:/home/ubuntu# kubectl delete pods testpod -n dev
pod "testpod" deleted
root@Master:/home/ubuntu# kubectl get pods -n dev
No resources found in dev namespace.
root@Master:/home/ubuntu#
```

4. To set a namespace for default: kubectl config set-context $(kubectl config current-context) --namespace=dev

```
root@Master:/home/ubuntu# kubectl config set-context $(kubectl config current-context) --namespace=dev
Context "minikube" modified.
root@Master:/home/ubuntu#
```

5. To view as to we are in which namespace: kubectl config view | grep namespace

```
root@Master:/home/ubuntu# kubectl config set-context $(kubectl config current-context) --namespace=dev
Context "minikube" modified.
root@Master:/home/ubuntu# kubectl config view | grep namespace
    namespace: dev
root@Master:/home/ubuntu#
```

17. Resource Quota

Description:

Request: A Request is the amount of that resources that the system will guarantee for the container and Kubernetes will use this value to decide on which node to place the pod.

Limit: A limit is the maximum amount of resources that Kubernetes will allow the container to use. In case if the request is not set for a container, it defaults to limits. If the limit is not set, it defaults to zero.

There can be 3 scenarios:

1. If Request and Limit, both are mentioned

    Then, we are good

2. If Request is not Mentioned and Limit is mentioned

    Then, Request = Limit

3. If Request is mentioned and limit is not mentioned

    Then, Limit = default

Namespaces can be assigned Resource Quota Objects, this will limit the amount of ways allowed to the objects to the objects in that namespace. Limit can be set on the below specified:

- Compute
- Memory
- Storage

There are two restrictions that a resource quota implies on a namespace:

- Every Container that runs in the namespace must have its own CPU limit.

- The total amount of CPU used by all containers in the namespace must not exceed a specified limit that is set on the namespace.

Commands:

Syntax:

apiVersion: v1

kind: Pod

metadata:

 name: resources

spec:

 containers:

 - name: resource

  image: centos

  command: ["/bin/bash", "-c", "while true; do echo Hello World; sleep 5 ; done"]

  resources:

   requests:

    memory: "64Mi"

    cpu: "100m"

   limits:

    memory: "128Mi"

    cpu: "200m"

1. Create a file: vi podresources.yaml
2. Create a pod in dev namespace: kubectl apply -f podresources.yaml -n dev
3. Check if the pod is created: kubectl get pods -n dev

```
root@Master:/home/ubuntu# kubectl apply -f podresources.yaml -n dev
pod/resources created
root@Master:/home/ubuntu# kubectl get pods -n dev
NAME        READY   STATUS    RESTARTS   AGE
resources   1/1     Running   0          7s
root@Master:/home/ubuntu#
```

4. Check the logs: kubectl describe pods resources -n dev

```
Events:
  Type    Reason     Age   From               Message
  ----    ------     ----  ----               -------
  Normal  Scheduled  82s   default-scheduler  Successfully assigned dev/resource
s to minikube
  Normal  Pulling    82s   kubelet            Pulling image "centos"
  Normal  Pulled     80s   kubelet            Successfully pulled image "centos"
 in 1.82918296s (1.829203309s including waiting)
  Normal  Created    80s   kubelet            Created container resource
  Normal  Started    80s   kubelet            Started container resource
root@Master:/home/ubuntu#
```

====RESOURCE QUOTA====

apiVersion: v1

kind: ResourceQuota

metadata:

  name: myquota

spec:

  hard:

    limits.cpu: "400m"

    limits.memory: "400Mi"

    requests.cpu: "200m"

    requests.memory: "200Mi"

1. Create a file: vi resourcequota.yaml
2. Create a pod: kubectl apply -f resourcequota.yaml -n dev
3. Check the pod: kubectl get pods -n dev

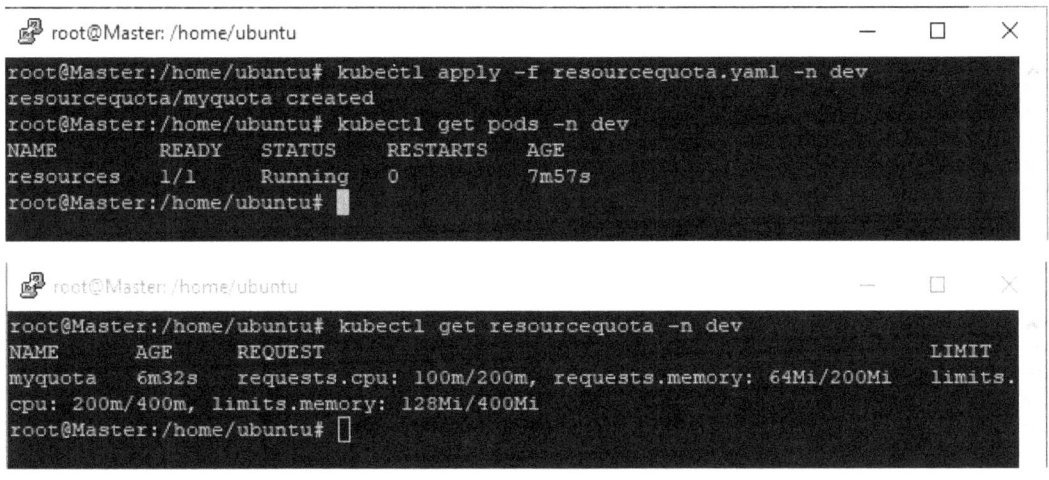

==

kind: Deployment

apiVersion: apps/v1

metadata:

  name: deployments

spec:

  replicas: 3

  selector:

    matchLabels:

      objtype: deployment

  template:

    metadata:

      name: testpod8

      labels:

        objtype: deployment

    spec:

    containers:

      - name: c00

        image: ubuntu

        command: ["/bin/bash", "-c", "while true; do echo Technical-Guftgu; sleep 5 ; done"]

        resources:

          requests:

            cpu: "200m"

1. **Set the Context to dev namespace:** kubectl config set-context $(kubectl config current-context) --namespace=dev

2. **Create a file:** vi testpod.yaml

3. **Create a pod:** kubectl apply -f testpod.yaml

```
root@Master:/home/ubuntu# kubectl apply -f testpod.yaml -n dev
deployment.apps/deployments created
root@Master:/home/ubuntu# kubectl get pods -n dev
NAME          READY   STATUS    RESTARTS   AGE
resources     1/1     Running   0          16m
root@Master:/home/ubuntu# kubectl config set-context $(kubectl config current-co
ntext) --namespace=dev
Context "minikube" modified.
root@Master:/home/ubuntu# kubectl apply -f testpod.yaml
deployment.apps/deployments unchanged
root@Master:/home/ubuntu# kubectl get pods
NAME          READY   STATUS    RESTARTS   AGE
resources     1/1     Running   0          17m
root@Master:/home/ubuntu# kubectl get deploy
NAME          READY   UP-TO-DATE   AVAILABLE   AGE
deployments   0/3     0            0           2m53s
root@Master:/home/ubuntu#
```

To specifiy a Limit Range:

```
apiVersion: v1
kind: LimitRange
metadata:
  name: cpu-limit-range
spec:
  limits:
  - default:
      cpu: 1
    defaultRequest:
      cpu: 0.5
    type: Container
```

When request is not mentioned but limit is mentioned: cpu2.yml

```
apiVersion: v1
kind: Pod
metadata:
  name: default-cpu-demo-2
spec:
  containers:
  - name: default-cpu-demo-2-ctr
    image: nginx
    resources:
      limits:
        cpu: "1"
```

Steps:

1. Create a file: vi cpu2.yaml

2. Create a pod: kubectl apply -f cpu2.yaml

3. Check if the pod is created: kubectl get pods default-cpu-demo-2

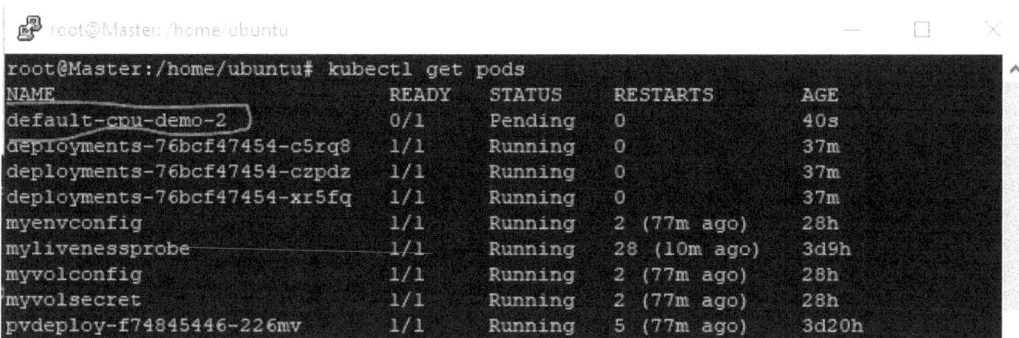

4. Check if the Request is equal to Limit: Kubectl describe pod default-cpu-demo-2

```
root@Master:/home/ubuntu# kubectl describe pods default-cpu-demo-2
Name:              default-cpu-demo-2
Namespace:         default
Priority:          0
Service Account:   default
Node:              <none>
Labels:            <none>
Annotations:       <none>
Status:            Pending
IP:
IPs:               <none>
Containers:
  default-cpu-demo-2-ctr:
    Image:      nginx
    Port:       <none>
    Host Port:  <none>
    Limits:
      cpu:  1
    Requests:
      cpu:       1
```

==

When Request is defined but Limit is not Defined: cpu3.yaml

==
===========================

apiVersion: v1

kind: Pod

metadata:

  name: default-cpu-demo-3

spec:

  containers:

  - name: default-cpu-demo-3-ctr

    image: nginx

    resources:

      requests:

        cpu: "0.75"

Steps:

1. Create a file: vi cpu3.yaml
2. Create a pod: kubectl apply -f cpu3.yaml
3. Check if the pod is created: kubectl get pods

Y

```
root@Master:/home/ubuntu# vi cpu3.yaml
root@Master:/home/ubuntu# kubectl apply -f cpu3.yaml
pod/default-cpu-demo-3 created
root@Master:/home/ubuntu# kubectl get pods
NAME                                READY   STATUS    RESTARTS       AGE
default-cpu-demo-2                  0/1     Pending   0              12m
default-cpu-demo-3                  0/1     Pending   0              8s
deployments-76bcf47454-c5rq8        1/1     Running   0              49m
deployments-76bcf47454-czpdz        1/1     Running   0              49m
deployments-76bcf47454-xr5fq        1/1     Running   0              49m
myenvconfig                         1/1     Running   2 (89m ago)    28h
mylivenessprobe                     1/1     Running   29 (5m11s ago) 3d9h
myvolconfig                         1/1     Running   2 (89m ago)    28h
myvolsecret                         1/1     Running   2 (89m ago)    28h
pvdeploy-f74845446-226mv            1/1     Running   5 (89m ago)    3d20h
root@Master:/home/ubuntu#
```

Note* In this case, the limit will be default: 1

18. Horizontal Pod Autoscaling

19. Kubernetes Jobs

20. Ingress Controller

Description: An Ingress Controller is a piece of software that provides reverse proxy, configurable traffic routing and TLS Termination. Kubernetes ingress resources are used to configure the ingress rules and routes for individual Kubernetes services. When you use an ingress controller and ingress rules, a single IP address can be used to route traffic to multiple services in a Kubernetes cluster.

Commands:

1. To view the Ingress Controller: kubectl get ingress
2. To delete the ingress controller: kubectl delete ingress <Ingress-Name>

We are going to use HELM3 to install NGINX Ingress Controller.

Basic Ingress Controller

NAMESPACE=ingress-basic

helm repo add ingress-nginx https://kubernetes.github.io/ingress-nginx

helm repo update

helm install ingress-nginx ingress-nginx/ingress-nginx \

  --create-namespace \

  --namespace $NAMESPACE \

  --set controller.service.annotations."service\.beta\.kubernetes\.io/azure-load-balancer-health-probe-request-path"=/healthz

Customized Ingress Controller

REGISTRY_NAME=customizedingressacr.azurecr.io

SOURCE_REGISTRY=registry.k8s.io

CONTROLLER_IMAGE=ingress-nginx/controller

CONTROLLER_TAG=v1.8.1

PATCH_IMAGE=ingress-nginx/kube-webhook-certgen

PATCH_TAG=v20230407

DEFAULTBACKEND_IMAGE=defaultbackend-amd64

DEFAULTBACKEND_TAG=1.5

az acr import --name $REGISTRY_NAME --source $SOURCE_REGISTRY/$CONTROLLER_IMAGE:$CONTROLLER_TAG --image $CONTROLLER_IMAGE:$CONTROLLER_TAG

az acr import --name $REGISTRY_NAME --source $SOURCE_REGISTRY/$PATCH_IMAGE:$PATCH_TAG --image $PATCH_IMAGE:$PATCH_TAG

az acr import --name $REGISTRY_NAME --source $SOURCE_REGISTRY/$DEFAULTBACKEND_IMAGE:$DEFAULTBACKEND_TAG --image $DEFAULTBACKEND_IMAGE:$DEFAULTBACKEND_TAG

Delete Ingress Controller

1. Identify Ingress Controller to delete

    To List the Ingress Controllers in current namespace : kubectl get ingress

2. Backup your configurationa

    To export the ingress configuration to yaml file: kubectl get ingress <ingress-name> -o yaml > backup.yaml

3. Delete the Ingress Controller: kubectl delete ingress <ingress-name>

4. Verify the deletion: kubectl get ingress

https://learn.microsoft.com/en-us/azure/aks/ingress-basic?tabs=azure-cli

21. HELM Chart

Description: HELP is a packaging Manager used for Automatic Installation, Helm Chart Versioning and Dependency Management. It is a Kubernetes equivalent of yum(Linux) and apt(Ubuntu) which helps in managing Kubernetes applications with Helm Charts. The charts can either be stored locally or fetched from remote chart repositories.

Why use Help: Writing and Managing Kubernetes YAML Manifests for all the required Kubernetes Objects can be time consuming for the simplest of deployments. We would need at least 3 YAML manifests with duplicated and hardcoded values. Helm simplifies this process and creates a single package that can be advertised to the cluster.

HELM Kubernetes automatically maintains a database of all volumes of our releases. So, whenever something goes wrong during deployment, rolling back to a previous version is just one command away.

Keywords

Helm Charts: A chard is a HELM Package which contains all of the resource definitions necessary to run an application, tool or service inside of a Kubernetes Cluster.

21.1 Commands

1. To list the chart Repositories: helm repo list
2. To create a new chart: helm create <chart name>
3. To add a chart repository: Helm repo add <Name> <URL>
4. To remove one or more chart repositories: Helm repo remove <Name>
5. To update information of available charts: helm repo update
6. To find a chart repository: helm search repo <chart>

7. To find information about a chart: helm show <values | chart | read me| all> (chart name)

8. To install a package: helm install <release name> <chart name>

9. To install Jenkins: Helm install <package name> ie helm install jenkins

21.2 Installation

$ curl -fsSL -o get_helm.sh https://raw.githubusercontent.com/helm/helm/main/scripts/get-helm-3

$ chmod 700 get_helm.sh

$ ./get_helm.sh

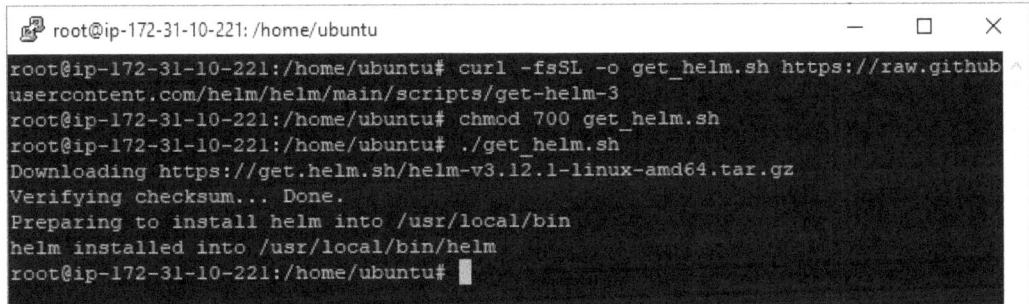

To verify the Installation: which helm

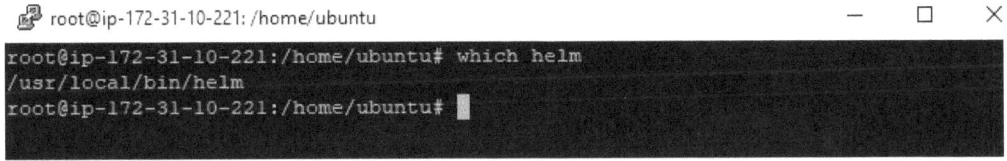

Now create First Helm Chart: helm repo add stable https://charts.helm.sh/stable

22. Kubernetes Migration

22.1 Discovery

This phase involves Identify your current infrastructure. Take an inventory of all your existing hardware and software components. This will help you understand your current environment and determine what needs to be migrated.

22.2 Assessment

Kubernetes allows businesses to deploy and manage containerized applications with ease, providing a strong foundation for microservices and cloud-native architectures. Kubernetes Migration can be simple by following a planned approach. It involves assessing the environment which includes understanding your current infrastructure, applications and workloads and determining how will they fit into a Kubernetes Environment.

The steps involved in assessment are:

- **Application Inventory:** Identify all the applications that will be migrated and determine their dependencies. You will need to ensure that all applications are compatible with Kubernetes and its associated tools.

- **Compatibility Testing:** Test the compatibility of your existing applications and systems with Kubernetes.

- **Dependency Mapping:** Creating a dependency map between applications, databases and other systems.

- **Containerization:** Containerizing your applications and systems before migrating to Kubernetes to ensure compatibility.

The various tools available for assessment are:

- Kubernetes Application Migration Toolkit (KAM): This tool helps to identify applications that are suitable for migration to Kubernetes and provides a roadmap for the migration process.

- Cloud-Native Application Assessment Tool: This tool provides a comprehensive analysis of your existing applications and infrastructure, identifying any potential issues or challenges that may arise during the migration process.

22.3 Planning

This phase involves defining the migration goals, creation of Project Plan which includes the activity details with timelines and creation of Migration Strategy.

22.4 Migration

Landing Zone Creation

The first step in executing your migration is to configure your Kubernetes Cluster. This involves setting up Kubernetes infrastructure and installing any necessary add-ons and tools. Some of the key activities are:

Sr. No	Activity	Person	Duration
1	Create Virtual Network	TBD	2
2	Create Subnets	TBD	2
3	Create NSG Rules	TBD	2
4	Create Application Gateway	TBD	4
5	Create Kubernetes Cluster	TBD	
6	Create Nodes and Add to the Cluster	TBD	4
7	Configure Networking	TBD	4
8	Install and configure Prometheus	TBD	4
9	Install and configure Grafana	TBD	4
10	Setup Storage	TBD	4

Workload Migration

The steps involved in workload migration are:

- Creating container images for your applications

- Creating Kubernetes manifests to define your applications and their dependencies.
- Deploying your application to Kubernetes
- Validating and Testing your Applications (UAT)

There are a variety of tools and strategies available to help you execute your migration to Kubernetes. Some of these include:

- Kubernetes migration tools like Velero, which can help you backup and restore your applications during the migration process
- Kubernetes deployment tools like Helm, which can help you automate the deployment of your applications to Kubernetes

Post Migration Considerations

After successfully migration your applications to Kubernetes, its important to keep the applications in Hypercare for 2 weeks to ensure we have a seamless migration. One important point is to evaluate the performance of applications of migrated applications. By implementing best practices for testing, optimization, and ongoing maintenance, businesses can ensure that their applications are running optimally in their new Kubernetes environment.

22.5 Optimize

Cost allocation: Kubernetes spend increases in direct proportion to the number of clusters, where apps and services are deployed, and how they are configured. Reporting the costs of multi tenant clusters and allocating costs to the correct owners can be challenging. Kubernetes deploys transient workloads that rely on both shared and external resources. Usage is measured in seconds, and tracking Kubernetes resources used by a workload can be difficult. As the Kubernetes environment grows, so does the number of clusters and nodes. Spending must be monitored to avoid wasting Kubernetes resources; therefore, platform engineering teams must be able to allocate and showback costs in a business-relevant context and create feedback loops with engineering to enable a culture of service ownership.

Resource labeling: Mapping costs to a Kubernetes component, such as a namespace or label, helps to properly allocate costs to individual business units.

The Kubernetes Vertical Pod Autoscaler (VPA) uses the historical memory and CPU usage of workloads together with the current usage of pods to generate recommendations for resource requests and limits. Node labels in Kubernetes allow you to label your nodes. You can configure pods to use specific "nodeSelectors" that match specific node labels, which determine which nodes a pod can be scheduled onto. Using instance groups of different instance types that are appropriately labeled allows you to match the underlying hardware available from your chosen public cloud or private cloud provider choice with your Kubernetes workloads. Without resource labeling, it is difficult to allocate costs appropriately and make informed decisions on costs, optimizations, and cloud spend.

Cost avoidance and optimization: Cost avoidance, per the FinOps Foundation, means to reduce usage and optimize costs to get a better cloud rate. Most of the actions required for cost avoidance are dependent on engineers. Platform engineering teams can avoid costs and increase optimization using Kubernetes by shipping applications more quickly, lowering costs by optimizing cloud usage, and reducing risks by implementing Kubernetes security features. Kubernetes governance can avoid costs and increase optimization by automatically enforcing policies built with security and cost in mind.

22.4.2 Governance

Kubernetes Governance is a set of policies and procedures organizations adopt to define how Kubernetes is managed and maintained. It includes management of Kubernetes resources, scheduling, upgrades, and role-based access control. It also includes the process for making decisions about Kubernetes, such as how to manage security issues, bug fixes, and feature requests.

The following five principles provide an excellent starting point for building your Kubernetes governance model:

- **Aligned with business objectives:** Kubernetes strategy should be an integral part of the overall business and IT strategy. All Kubernetes systems and policies must be shown to support business goals.

- **Collaboration:** There must be clear agreements between Kubernetes infrastructure owners and other stakeholders to ensure that Kubernetes is being used appropriately and effectively.

- **Change management:** All changes to Kubernetes environments must be implemented consistently and according to Kubernetes best practices, aligning with the appropriate organizational controls.

- **Dynamic response:** Kubernetes governance should rely on monitoring, tooling, and policy automation to effectively manage the Kubernetes environment.

- **Policies and standards compliance:** Kubernetes usage standards must align with relevant regulations and compliance standards used within your organization and by others in your industry.

Kubernetes governance is the process of setting policies, standards, and procedures that function as guardrails to ensure the security, compliance, and cost-effective use of Kubernetes within an organization. Kubernetes Governance includes the following:

- **Creating a Kubernetes Governance Team:** Assemble a team of experts who understand Kubernetes and the organization's needs, including members from the development, operations, security, and compliance teams.

- **Establishing Policies and Standards:** Establish policies and standards for the use of Kubernetes, particularly security, compliance, and cost-effectiveness.

- **Developing Processes and Guidelines:** Develop processes and guidelines to verify that the governance policies and standards have been successfully implemented, including approval and communication processes.

- **Monitoring and Enforcing Policies:** Monitor and enforce the policies and standards to make certain that they are being followed; implementing tooling and automation to enforce Kubernetes guardrails reduces the challenges inherent in complex Kubernetes environments.

- **Reviewing and Updating:** Review and update the policies, standards, and processes regularly to confirm that they still meet the organization's needs as they change over time.

23. Policies

In general, organizations may deploy both cluster-wide and namespace-specific (or application-specific) policies. Cluster-wide policies tend to apply to all workloads and may cover security, efficiency, and reliability categories. These are general rules-of-thumb, and exceptions may be granted on an instance-by-instance basis between the Platform and Security teams.

Cluster wide Polices

- Memory requests should be set
- CPU requests should be set
- Liveness probes should be set
- Readiness probes should be set
- Image pull policy should be "Always"
- Container should not have dangerous capabilities

Namespace policies

Namespace policies are below specified:

o Container should not have insecure capabilities
o Host IPC should not be configured
o Host PID should not be configured
o Privilege escalation should not be allowed
o Should not be running as privileged
o Image tag should be specified.
o Namespace quotas should be set

24. Kubernetes Security

Infrastructure as Code scanning: Infrastructure as code (IaC) enables the use of a configuration language to provision and manage infrastructure. This applies the repeatability, transparency, and testing of modern software development to infrastructure management. The primary goal of IaC is to reduce error and configuration drift, which allows engineers to focus on higher value tasks. Making use of IaC provides significant benefits for Kubernetes users, such as reduced human error, repeatability and consistency, improved change tracking, and disaster recovery. Infrastructure as code scanning is the ability to scan IaC files against a set of policies and Kubernetes best practices, which helps an organization ensure alignment with Kubernetes governance goals, such as application security, reliability, and cost.

Container image scanning: Containers enable development teams to build, package, and deploy applications and services to diverse environments and deployment targets, therefore securing and protecting the integrity of containers is critical to organizations building and deploying in cloud-native environments. Containers are built on a base image, which is the starting point for Linux containers. A vulnerability in your base image will exist in every container that contains that base image. Finding a trusted source for your base image, staying up to date with patches, controlling permissions, and limiting the use of additional images that are not required for deployment to production can help increase the security of your container images. It is still critical to scan images and detect misconfigurations because Common Vulnerabilities and Exposures (CVEs) can be introduced at any time. Scanning containers and all their components to identify security vulnerabilities is a critical component of container security, and therefore an important aspect of Kubernetes governance.

Securing Kubernetes Hosts : Kubernetes can be deployed in different ways: on bare metal, on-premise, and in the public cloud (a custom Kubernetes build on virtual machines OR use a managed service). Since Kubernetes is designed to be highly portable, customers can easily and migrate their workloads and switch between multiple installations.

Because Kubernetes can be designed to fit a large variety of scenarios, this flexibility is a weakness when it comes to securing Kubernetes clusters. The engineers responsible for deploying the Kubernetes platform must know about all the potential attack vectors and vulnerabilities for their clusters.

To harden the underlying hosts for Kubernetes clusters, we recommend that you install the latest version of the operating systems, harden the operating systems, implement necessary patch management and configuration management systems, implement essential firewall rules and undertake specific datacenter-based security measures.

Securing Kubernetes Components:

Securing Kubernetes Cluster components includes:

- Securing the Kubernetes Dashboard
- Restricting access to etcd (Important)
- Controlling network access to sensitive ports
- Controlling access to the Kubernetes API
- Implementing role-based access control in Kubernetes
- Limiting access to Kubelets
- Controlling Network Access to Sensitive Ports
- Controlling access to Kubernetes API

Implementing Role based access control in Kubernetes

Role-based access control (RBAC) is a method for regulating access to computer or network resources based on the roles of individual users within your organization. Fortunately, Kubernetes comes with an integrated Role-Based Access Control (RBAC) component with default roles that allow you to define user responsibilities depending on what actions a client might want to perform. You should use the Node and RBAC authorizers together in combination with the NodeRestriction admission plugin.

The RBAC component matches an incoming user or group to a set of permissions linked to roles. These permissions combine verbs (get, create, delete) with resources (pods, services, nodes) and can be namespace or cluster scoped. RBAC authorization uses the rbac.authorization.k8s.io API group to drive authorization decisions, allowing you to dynamically configure policies through the Kubernetes API.

To enable RBAC, start the API server with the --authorization-mode flag set to a comma-separated list that includes RBAC; for example:

kube-apiserver --authorization-mode=Example,RBAC --other-options --more-options

Kubernetes Security Best Practices

Container Image: A container image (CI) is an immutable, lightweight, standalone, executable package of software that includes everything needed to run an application: code, runtime, system tools, system libraries and settings [https://www.docker.com/resources/what-container]. Each image shares the kernel of the operating system present in the host machine.

Your CIs must be built on a approved and secure base image. This base image must be scanned and monitored at regular intervals to ensure that all CIs are based on a secure and authentic image. Implement strong governance policies that determine how images are built and stored in trusted image registries.

- Only use authorized images in Your environment
- Use A CI Pipeline To Control and Identify Vulnerabilities
- Minimize Features in All CIs
- Use distroless or empty images when possible
- Implement continuous security vulnerability scanning
- Apply security context to your pods and containers
- Continuously assess the privileges used by containers

25. Service Mesh

A service mesh is an infrastructure layer that can handle communications between services in applications quickly, securely and reliably, which can help reduce the complexity of managing microservices and deployments. They provide a uniform way to secure, connect and monitor microservices. and a service mesh is great at resolving operational challenges and issues when running those containers and microservices.

www.ingramcontent.com/pod-product-compliance
Lightning Source LLC
LaVergne TN
LVHW070528070526
838199LV00073B/6729